OLYMPIC SPORTS

OLYMPIC BASKETBALL

BY LUKE HANLON

SportsZone

An Imprint of Abdo Publishing
abdobooks.com

abdobooks.com

Published by Abdo Publishing, a division of ABDO, PO Box 398166, Minneapolis, Minnesota 55439.

Printed in the United States of America, North Mankato, Minnesota.
102024
012025

THIS BOOK CONTAINS
RECYCLED MATERIALS

Cover Photo: Gregory Shamus/Getty Images Sport/Getty Images
Interior Photos: Jed Jacobsohn/Getty Images Sport/Getty Images, 5; Steve Dykes/Getty Images Sport/Getty Images, 7; Tony Marshall/EMPICS/PA Images/Getty Images, 8; Streeter Lecka/Getty Images Sport/Getty Images, 10, 39; Filippo Monteforte/AFP/Getty Images, 12; Bettmann/Getty Images, 15, 27; Wolff & Tritschler/ullstein bild/Getty Images, 16; Rich Clarkson/Rich Clarkson & Assoc./NCAA Photos/Getty Images, 17, 28; Joe Patronite/Getty Images Sport/Getty Images, 18; Icon Sportswire/Getty Images, 21; Sepia Times/Universal Images Group/Getty Images, 23; Tim Clary/AFP/Getty Images, 24; Wally McNamee/Corbis Historical/Getty Images, 30; AP Images, 33; Jed Jacobsohn/Allsport/Getty Images Sport/Getty Images, 35; Don Emmert/AFP/Getty Images, 37; Ezra Shaw/Getty Images Sport/Getty Images, 40; Tim Clayton/Corbis Sport/Getty Images, 42; Mike Ehrmann/Getty Images Sport/Getty Images, 44; Damien Meyer/AFP/Getty Images, 45

Editor: Haley Williams
Series Designer: Karli Kruse

Library of Congress Control Number: 2024938387

Publisher's Cataloging-in-Publication Data

Names: Hanlon, Luke, author.
Title: Olympic basketball / by Luke Hanlon
Description: Minneapolis, Minnesota: ABDO Publishing, 2025 | Series: Olympic sports | Includes online resources and index.
Identifiers: ISBN 9781098295479 (lib. bdg.) | ISBN 9798384916475 (ebook)
Subjects: LCSH: Olympic games--Juvenile literature. | Basketball--Juvenile literature. | Olympians (Olympic athletes)--Juvenile literature. | Olympics--History--Juvenile literature. | Sports--Juvenile literature.
Classification: DDC 796.332--dc23

TABLE OF CONTENTS

CHAPTER 1

THE REDEEM TEAM

Less than four minutes remained in the men's basketball gold-medal game at the 2008 Olympics in Beijing, China. The United States led Spain by seven points. The Americans seemed to be on their way to the top of the podium. But Spain refused to back down.

Rudy Fernandez grabbed a rebound for Spain. The guard then set up the team's offense. Carlos Jimenez eventually passed the ball to power forward Pau Gasol on the left wing. Gasol knocked down a jump shot. Just like that, the Americans' lead was cut to five points. They needed a response, and fast.

LOSING IS NOT AN OPTION

The United States has a proud history in Olympic basketball. But the US men's team arrived at the 2008 Games with a point to prove. The previous Olympics had been four years earlier in Athens, Greece. It was a forgettable experience for

Team USA's Kobe Bryant, *left*, and Spain's Pau Gasol, *right*, compete in the men's basketball gold-medal game at the 2008 Olympics.

the Americans. They lost two games in group play and barely made the quarterfinals. A narrow victory against Spain sent Team USA to the semifinals. But there, Argentina stunned the United States 89–81. The Americans returned home with a bronze medal. It equaled their worst finish in Olympic basketball history.

Men's basketball has been an Olympic sport since 1936. The United States won the first seven gold medals when the competition was limited to amateurs. Then, at the 1992 Games in Barcelona, Spain, professional basketball players began competing in the Olympics. That year, the United States formed the "Dream Team." The roster, packed with future Hall of Famers, inspired countries around the world to care more about basketball.

Entering the 2004 Games, the United States had an overall record of 109–2 in Olympic play. The country's top players had started taking the Olympics less seriously. Many of them just assumed they would win. And some star players even turned down the opportunity to play. Losing three times in the 2004 Olympic tournament shook the US program to its core. Changes were needed. And USA Basketball, which runs the national teams, set out to make them.

The rebuilding of USA Basketball started at the top. Jerry Colangelo had enjoyed a respected career in the National

Basketball Association (NBA) as the general manager for the Phoenix Suns. In April 2005, USA Basketball brought him in to run the men's program. His first move was hiring Mike Krzyzewski to coach the team.

Krzyzewski, or Coach K as he was better known, had built Duke University into a men's college basketball powerhouse. Few coaches in the game commanded more respect. With clear leaders established, Colangelo and Krzyzewski began recruiting players for Team USA.

The 1992 Dream Team outscored its opponents by an average of almost 44 points per game.

Mike Krzyzewski coached the US men's national basketball team from 2005 to 2016.

In years past, players showed up for a training camp for just a few weeks before the Olympics to prepare. For the lead-up to Beijing, however, the US team asked players to commit for three years. That meant participating in training camps and international tournaments each summer. Colangelo wanted the top superstars to treat the Olympics as seriously as they did the NBA.

Some of the NBA's brightest stars committed right away. LeBron James, Dwyane Wade, and Carmelo Anthony all returned from the 2004 Olympic team. Kobe Bryant proved to be the key addition to the roster, though. The Los Angeles Lakers shooting guard was already a three-time NBA champion.

He had led the league in scoring for two straight seasons heading into the summer of 2007.

However, some people questioned if Bryant would be willing to share the stage with James. Both Bryant and James were ball-dominant superstars. And after James led the Cleveland Cavaliers to the 2007 NBA Finals, many started calling him the world's best player. People wondered whether the ultra-competitive Bryant would accept being teammates with James.

Those doubts quickly washed away. Bryant and James were among those who joined Team USA at the 2007 Americas Championship. That tournament featured the best teams from North, South, and Central America. The US players showed that they were committed as they cruised to an undefeated record and tournament championship.

The US team's performance at the Americas Championship showed that the NBA superstars

MORE THAN BASKETBALL

Mike Krzyzewski took the responsibility of coaching the US men's basketball team very seriously. He played basketball at the United States Military Academy from 1966 to 1969. Coach K wanted his players to know what it meant to represent their country. During training camp before the Olympics, Coach K had military members talk to the US players about their service. Some players said that gave them added motivation to play their best for Team USA.

could put their egos aside and focus on winning. And they kept it up once the 2008 Olympics began the following summer in Beijing. After three blowout wins, the Americans faced Spain

Kobe Bryant, *right*, averaged 15.0 points per game and led the United States with 17 three-pointers during the 2008 Olympics.

in the group stage. During the NBA season, Bryant and Gasol played together on the Lakers. Gasol was like a brother to Bryant. But Bryant wanted his US teammates to know that Gasol was just another opponent in the Olympics. Gasol set a screen early in the game against the United States. Instead of trying to avoid Gasol, Bryant forcefully ran him over. Bryant's teammates knew he came to compete. And the Americans went on to beat Spain 119–82.

Many people considered those two teams to be the best in the world. And a few days later, they met again in the gold-medal game. The United States had faced little adversity on its way to the final. Spain got there by narrowly defeating Lithuania in the semifinals. Having already lost to the United States earlier in the tournament, Spain came into the game as a massive underdog. But Spain's team chemistry flourished in the championship meeting. And behind hot shooting performances, Spain kept the game tight throughout.

REDEMPTION

Spain cut the Americans' lead down to five points with 3:25 left. The momentum had completely shifted in Spain's favor. On the next possession, US point guard Chris Paul set up the offense. Facing a zone defense, the Americans worked the ball around the perimeter. Then Wade drove hard into the paint

Members of the US men's basketball team celebrate after winning gold at the 2008 Olympics.

and drew four defenders near him. Instead of forcing a shot, the guard passed to an open Bryant across the court.

Fernandez closed out on Bryant quickly. But Bryant did not panic. He jab-stepped toward Fernandez. Then he rose up for a three-pointer. Fernandez jumped in an attempt to block Bryant's shot. Instead, Fernandez hit Bryant's shooting arm after he released the ball. The ball hit nothing but net to give Bryant the chance at a four-point play. After the shot went in, Bryant raised his left index finger to his lips to shush the pro-Spain crowd. He then made a free throw to put the United States up by nine.

Those were four of Bryant's 13 points in the fourth quarter. On a team full of superstars, the veteran presence of Bryant proved to be the difference for the United States. The Americans closed out the game and won 118–107 to claim the gold medal. Four years after one of the lowest moments in USA Basketball's history, the 2008 team helped restore the country's status as a powerhouse at the Olympics. While the 1992 Games gave basketball fans the Dream Team, the 2008 US squad would forever be known as the Redeem Team.

CHAPTER 2

THE GAME GOES GLOBAL

In 1891, James Naismith invented the game of basketball. He introduced the sport to his gym class at a school in Springfield, Massachusetts. Basketball quickly spread across the United States. The school also had multiple international students. They helped bring the sport to their home countries.

By 1904, the Olympic Games were still very new. The first modern Olympics had been held just eight years earlier in Athens. For the 1904 Games in St. Louis, Olympic organizers wanted to showcase basketball to the world. However, no medals were awarded. Three college men's teams played games on an outdoor clay court that got soaked in the rain.

Men's basketball became an official Olympic sport at the 1936 Games in Berlin, Germany. Since the game was invented in the United States, the Americans came into the tournament as heavy favorites. They had years of experience, whereas their opponents were just getting started. The United States also

James Naismith used elements of several outdoor sports, including soccer and football, to create the sport of basketball.

Twenty-one men's teams from around the world competed in the first Olympic basketball tournament in 1936.

had much taller players than its opponents. Once again playing on muddy outdoor courts, the United States won the sport's first Olympic gold medal.

STOLEN VICTORY

The American dominance was a sign of things to come. In the first seven Olympics with men's basketball, the Americans won all 55 games they played. They expected a similar result at the 1972 Games in Munich, West Germany.

The United States reached the gold-medal game again that year. The Americans just needed to beat the Soviet Union to keep the winning streak alive. However, the Soviets had a key advantage. During this time, only amateur athletes could compete at the Olympics. To get around this rule, the Soviet government registered the country's pro athletes as military members. This meant the Soviet players were essentially professionals. In comparison, the United States relied on college players.

The Soviets controlled most of the gold-medal game. But with only three seconds left, US guard Doug Collins went to

Doug Collins of the United States shoots a free throw during the 1972 Olympic gold-medal game against the Soviet Union.

the free-throw line with his team down by one. He calmly sank both shots to give the United States a 50–49 lead.

On the Soviet inbound pass, the referees stopped the game with one second left. The Soviet coach claimed he called a timeout before Collins's second free throw. The refs reset the

The Soviet Union men's basketball team won its ninth Olympic medal at the 1988 Games in Seoul, South Korea.

game clock to three seconds and let the Soviets inbound the ball again. A Soviet player heaved a long shot that did not get close to the basket. The American bench spilled onto the court to celebrate winning gold.

However, their celebrations were cut short. The scorer's table had accidentally reset the clock to 50 seconds before the play. Despite protests from the American coaches and players, the refs reset the clock to three seconds. This time, the Soviets sailed a full-court pass to 6-foot, 7-inch Aleksandr Belov. As Belov caught the pass, his defender fell to the floor. Belov scored an open layup to win gold.

For the first time in Olympic men's basketball history, the United States had lost a game. Though the final score favored the Soviets, the American players felt the gold medal was stolen from them. When it came time for the medal ceremony, the Americans refused to stand on the podium. To this day, no one from the 1972 US team has accepted their silver medal.

DREAM TEAM

The United States bounced back after the controversial loss in 1972. The Americans won gold in 1976 and 1984. They likely would have won at the 1980 Games in Moscow, Soviet Union, as well. However, the United States boycotted the Olympics that year. This was because the Soviet Union had invaded

Afghanistan in late 1979. Since the 1980 Games were being held in the Soviet Union, the United States, along with about 60 other countries, protested the invasion by not competing in the Olympics. The Soviets responded by leading a boycott of the 1984 Games in Los Angeles.

By the 1988 Olympics in Seoul, South Korea, both powers were back. The Soviets defeated the Americans in the semifinals. There was no controversy this time. The Soviet "amateur" players were simply better than the American college kids.

Over the years, the International Olympic Committee (IOC) began relaxing some of its rules about professional athletes. Ahead of the 1988 Olympics, each sport could decide whether to allow pro athletes. After the defeat in 1988, USA Basketball wanted to be on an even playing field with the Soviets. NBA commissioner David Stern also stated that players from his league should be allowed to play in the Olympics. The IOC granted his wish before the 1992 Games.

Almost all the world's best players were in the NBA during that time. And most of them were American. The 1992 US men's basketball team had 12 players. Eleven of them ended up making the Naismith Memorial Basketball Hall of Fame. Highlighted by superstars Michael Jordan, Magic Johnson, and Larry Bird, this squad became known as the Dream Team.

Although Michael Jordan, *left*, was the 1992 Dream Team's biggest attraction, Charles Barkley, *right*, led the team in scoring by averaging 18.0 points across eight games.

The Dream Team was a sensation in Barcelona during the 1992 Games. International fans had never gotten the chance to see the NBA's best players in person before. Fans followed the players around the country. Even the team's opponents were in awe of their competition. Some opposing players asked for photos and autographs from the NBA stars after they lost to the United States.

The outcome of the Dream Team's games was never in question. The team steamrolled over every opponent to win gold. In fact, US head coach Chuck Daly did not use a single timeout during the tournament. Coaches typically use timeouts to calm their team down or to stop a run by the opposing team.

The Dream Team won games by so much that Daly just let his team play. Having NBA superstars in the Olympics helped lift the popularity of basketball around the world. Future NBA stars such as Germany's Dirk Nowitzki, Spain's Pau Gasol, and France's Tony Parker all said they wanted to play basketball professionally because of the Dream Team.

WOMEN JOIN THE GAME

Less than a year after Naismith invented basketball, women began playing the sport as well. In 1896, Stanford University and the University of California played the first women's college basketball game. But many people at the time believed it was not proper for women to compete in sports.

Forty years after men's basketball became an Olympic sport, women's basketball made its debut at the 1976 Games in Montreal, Canada. Although the United States had a long history with the sport, the Soviet Union came into the first tournament as the team to beat. With three players standing 6-foot-4 or taller, the Soviets cruised to an undefeated record to win gold. With the Americans boycotting the 1980 Games, an almost unchanged Soviet roster won gold again in Moscow.

The US women's basketball team broke through for its first gold in 1984. Women's college basketball was gaining support and popularity in the country during that time. This helped

Women did not start playing in international basketball tournaments until 1953.

the United States become a force at the Games. The Americans won gold again in 1988. However, their run at the top was short-lived. By 1992, the Soviet Union had broken into several smaller countries. Athletes from those former Soviet nations played on what was known as the Unified Team. The United Team defeated the United States in the semifinals at the 1992 Games. The Americans went on to win the bronze medal.

Atlanta was set to host the 1996 Olympics. With four years to prepare for the Games on home soil, the Americans knew that settling for bronze would not be good enough. Almost a

Lisa Leslie, *right*, led the US women's basketball team to four Olympic gold medals between 1996 and 2008.

year before the 1996 Olympics kicked off, the US women's team began a promotional world tour. The Americans played games against their top international rivals. They also played against top college teams. Featuring future basketball Hall of Famers such as Lisa Leslie and Sheryl Swoopes, the US team won all 52 of its games on the tour.

The US women continued their domination at the 1996 Olympics. The Americans won all eight of their games by 15 or more points. That included a 111–87 win against Brazil in the gold-medal game in front of a crowd of nearly 33,000 fans. The 1996 team set the standard for US women's basketball going forward.

Since those Games, many superstars of the Women's National Basketball Association (WNBA) have added to their legacies by representing the United States in the Olympics. Legends Sue Bird, Sylvia Fowles, and Diana Taurasi helped the US women create a seemingly unstoppable Olympic dynasty. Modern stars Brittney Griner, Breanna Stewart, and A'ja Wilson have continued to carry on that tradition as well. Those three helped the United States win its eighth straight Olympic gold medal at the 2024 Games in Paris, France. That triumph extended the US women's Olympic win streak to 61 games.

THREE-ON-THREE

The biggest change in recent Olympic basketball history came in 2017. That year, the IOC voted to add three-on-three basketball to the Games. Three-on-three games are played on a half court. Games last either 10 minutes or until a team scores 21 points. Shots inside the arc are worth one point, and shots behind the arc are worth two. At the 2024 Olympics in Paris, France, Germany won the women's three-on-three gold. On the men's side, the Netherlands topped the podium.

CHAPTER 3

INTERNATIONAL ICONS

From the start, the United States established itself as the team to beat in Olympic basketball. Even when only amateurs could play, the Americans boasted several talented teams. But none were as star-studded as the 1960 US men's team. That squad is considered the greatest amateur basketball team ever assembled.

The team ran a fast-paced offense led by guards Jerry West and Oscar Robertson. Both West and Robertson could score with ease. And they each liked to share the ball as well. They are regarded as two of the best basketball players of all time. Robertson scored 17 points per game in the 1960 Olympic tournament in Rome, Italy. That tied him for the team lead with Jerry Lucas. The 6-foot-8 Lucas was one of the youngest players on the team at 20 years old. But the forward played his best in the biggest moments. Lucas led the United States in scoring in both medal-round games.

Jerry West, *left*, and Oscar Robertson were key players in the US men's undefeated run at the 1960 Olympics.

The Soviet Union's Aleksandr Belov goes up for a shot during the gold-medal game against the United States at the 1972 Olympics.

The Americans scored more than 100 points five times in the 1960 tournament. They also held their opponents to fewer than 60 points per game. The silver-medal winning Soviet Union gave the Americans their toughest game. But the United States still won by 24 points.

SOVIETS STEAL THE SHOW

The Soviet Union posed the biggest threat to the United States in the early years of Olympic basketball. From 1952 to 1980, the

Soviets ended every tournament with at least a bronze medal. Their shining moment came in 1972 when Aleksandr Belov scored at the buzzer to controversially beat the Americans and secure the gold medal.

Belov did more than just score the clutch bucket in 1972, though. The center led the Soviet Union in scoring with 14.4 points per game in that tournament. Then in the 1976 bronze-medal game, he recorded the first triple-double in Olympic basketball history.

Aleksandr Belov's teammate Sergei Belov ran the offense of that 1972 team. Sergei had flashy dribbling and passing skills. He was also a highly intelligent player who directed the well-drilled Soviet offense. And when the Soviets needed him most, Sergei stepped up. He scored a game-high 20 points in the 1972 gold-medal game. The 1972 Olympics marked the second of four that Sergei played in for the Soviet Union. He led the team to three bronze medals and one gold.

GOING PRO

Eight years before the Dream Team took over Barcelona, guard Michael Jordan put on a show in Los Angeles, California. Jordan, a student at the University of North Carolina at the time, dazzled the hometown crowd in the 1984 Olympics with his gravity-defying dunks and acrobatic layups. The guard also made a huge impression on the US head coach Bob Knight. Knight rarely gave his players praise. However, he called Jordan the greatest basketball player he had ever seen.

Jordan went pro after the 1984 Games. Since professional basketball players were not allowed at the 1988 Games, Jordan had to wait until 1992 to make his return to the Olympics. On a team packed with individual talent that year, Jordan proved

Michael Jordan ended his Olympic career with 256 points, 54 assists, and 45 steals across 16 games.

to be the United States' brightest star. He led the Americans with 21 points in the semifinals and added 22 more in the gold-medal game.

At 6-foot-6, Charles Barkley was undersized for a power forward. But he used his strength to rack up rebounds and score in the post. That showed in two trips to the Olympics. Despite the 1992 team having many all-time great scorers, Barkley led the squad with 18 points per game. Then he returned in 1992 and led the team in scoring again.

While the US men commanded the medal podium, other international stars emerged during this time. Despite standing 6 feet, 8 inches tall, Brazilian Oscar Schmidt had the skills of a guard. Schmidt scored 23 points in his Olympic debut in 1980. And he never slowed down from there. Schmidt averaged at least 24 points per game in five Olympic appearances for Brazil. His shining moment came when he scored 55 points against Spain in 1988. Through the 2024 Games, no player has ever scored more in a single Olympic game. And no man has scored more than Schmidt's 1,093 career points at the Olympics.

DUNK OF DEATH

Vince Carter was the leading scorer on the US men's team at the 2000 Olympics in Sydney, Australia. But one moment from those Games sticks out more than any other. In a group-play game against France, Carter stole a pass and drove hard to the basket. French center Frédéric Weis tried to take a charge. But Carter jumped over the 7-foot-2 Weis and threw down a vicious dunk. The French media called the play the "Dunk of Death."

GIANT IMPACT

No one could stop the Soviet Union's Uljana Semjonova at the first Olympic women's basketball tournament in 1972. The towering 7-foot center used her size to overpower opponents and help her team win gold. At the 1976 Games in Montreal, the United States posed the biggest threat to the Soviets. When the two teams met in the final, Semjonova took over the game with 32 points and 19 rebounds. The Soviets beat the United States 112–77.

After averaging a double-double in the 1976 Games, Semjonova played even better in 1980. In front of a home crowd, Semjonova averaged 21.8 points, 12.5 rebounds, and 2.8 blocks per game. And she showed up in the biggest game once again. She recorded 27 points and 21 rebounds in the gold-medal game against Bulgaria to help the Soviets repeat as Olympic champions.

AMERICANS TAKE OVER

Although basketball had been invented in the United States, the US women's team needed some time to develop into an Olympic power in the sport. By the 1980s, the Americans had gained a young star to help finally put them over the top. Teresa Edwards, a 20-year-old point guard from the University of Georgia, provided a defensive spark to help

Uljana Semjonova (10) was a key member of the Soviet women's team during the 1976 and 1980 Olympics.

the 1984 US team break through for gold on home soil in Los Angeles. That made her the youngest medalist in Olympic women's basketball history.

By the 1988 Games, Edwards had developed into one of the United States' best players. She helped the US women secure gold again in 1988 and bronze at the 1992 Games. Edwards had a knack for finding open teammates. The guard's passing skills were on full display at her fourth Olympics in 1996, where she recorded 64 assists. No player had ever had that many assists in a single Olympic tournament before.

Edwards had plenty of talented teammates to pass to in 1996. She was one of six players to later be inducted into the Naismith Memorial Basketball Hall of Fame. However, no player had a greater impact than Lisa Leslie. The 6-foot-5 center could control a game in the paint on offense and defense. Leslie could also dribble like a guard and finish at the rim with either hand. Her combination of size and skill helped her score a team-high 19.5 points per game in 1996. That year, she won the first of four career gold medals.

Australia made its first big impact in women's international basketball when it won bronze at the 1996 Games. Playing in front of a home crowd in Sydney four years later, the Australians felt like they could improve on that result. Lauren Jackson was the main reason why. The 6-foot-5 forward could

Members of Australia's women's basketball team salute the home crowd after winning silver at the 2000 Olympics.

score both inside and outside the paint. Jackson's elite scoring ability lifted Australia to silver at the 2000 Games.

In her five Olympic appearances, Jackson helped Australia win three silvers and two bronzes. Through the 2024 Games, no woman has scored more than her 581 points or grabbed more than her 285 rebounds at the Olympics.

CHAPTER 4

MODERN LEGENDS

After cruising to gold in 1992 and 1996, the US men just snuck past Lithuania 85–83 in the 2000 Olympic semifinals. The Americans then went on to defeat France by 10 points in the gold-medal game. But those Olympics showed that other countries were rapidly catching up with the United States.

That harsh reality hit the United States hard at the 2004 Games. The Americans lost twice in the group stage, falling to Puerto Rico and Lithuania. But it was Argentina that officially ended Team USA's run atop the podium. The United States had no answer for Manu Ginóbili. Already a star in the NBA, Ginóbili was not fazed by the Americans. The 6-foot-6 shooting guard made nine of his 13 shots and scored a game-high 29 points to lead Argentina to victory.

Argentina's upset of the United States stunned international basketball fans. But the win would not mean as much to the Argentinians if they did not come home with a gold medal.

Argentina's Manu Ginóbili, *center*, drives to the basket during a game against Spain at the 2004 Olympics.

Playing Italy in the gold-medal game, Argentina relied on Ginóbili and his teammate Luis Scola. Scola overpowered the Italians in the paint. The muscular forward finished with a game-high 25 points and 11 rebounds to lead Argentina to an 84–69 victory and its first Olympic basketball gold medal. Ginóbili and Scola then helped lead Argentina to a bronze medal at the 2008 Games.

By 2008, Spain had become the newest team to beat in international basketball. Power forward Pau Gasol propelled Spain's success. Gasol had a complete offensive game. At 7-feet tall, he had amazing footwork for a big man. He could score both from inside and by hitting mid-range jump shots. He was also one of the best passing big men in basketball history. In his first four Olympics, Gasol averaged at least 18 points per game. And he led Spain to silver medals in 2008 and 2012.

GOLDEN AGAIN

The Redeem Team in 2008 changed how US men's players approached the Olympics. Having Kobe Bryant on the team helped turn the United States back into a powerhouse. Bryant's fierce competitiveness rubbed off on the rest of his teammates. Even in team practices, Bryant would dive on the floor for loose balls. And in games, he could take over on the offensive end at any point.

Spain's Pau Gasol, *right*, and the United States' Dwight Howard, *second to right*, jump for the ball at the start of the 2008 Olympic men's final.

LeBron James was only 19 when he made his Olympic debut in 2004. Surrounded by Bryant and other elite teammates in 2008, James flourished. At 6 feet, 8 inches and 250 pounds, James could punish defenders on his way to the rim. If multiple defenders tried to pressure him, James was able to find open

LeBron James, *right*, averaged 15.5 points per game at the 2008 Olympics and 13.3 at the 2012 Games.

teammates with ease. His skills were on full display at the 2012 Olympic quarterfinals in London, England. James finished the game against Australia with a triple-double of 11 points, 14 rebounds, and 12 assists.

Another US star became the team's main option in the 2012 Games. Despite standing 6-foot-11, Kevin Durant played both in and out of the paint. The forward used his height to take jump shots over smaller defenders from anywhere on the floor. Durant led the United States in scoring in 2012, 2016, and 2021. And he scored at least 29 points in each gold-medal game win.

Both Durant and James returned to the Olympic stage in 2024. At 39 years old, James hadn't slowed down with age.

He ran the US offense and routinely set up his teammates to score. Meanwhile, a 35-year-old Durant made more than half his three-point attempts in Paris. The legendary duo helped the Americans win their fifth straight gold medal. James was also named the most valuable player of the tournament.

DOMINANT DUO

Once the US women won gold in 1996, they never looked back. Not only did the Americans routinely win gold after that, but they usually did it with ease. Having consistent performances from superstar players set the US standard of play. No two players better symbolized that standard than guards Sue Bird and Diana Taurasi.

After playing together at the University of Connecticut for two years, a 23-year-old Bird and a 22-year-old Taurasi made their Olympic debuts in 2004. Their roles with the US team

SLOVENIAN SENSATION

By the time the Tokyo Olympics in 2021 kicked off, Luka Dončić had become one of the NBA's best players. Fans around the world were anticipating what the Slovenian guard would do on the biggest international stage. In his Olympic debut, Dončić scored 48 points in a win against Argentina. Only Oscar Schmidt had scored more in an Olympic game. Dončić averaged 23.8 points, 9.7 rebounds, and 9.5 assists in the tournament. And he led Slovenia to a fourth-place finish in its first Olympic basketball appearance.

grew larger with each passing tournament. By the 2012 Games, the duo ran the team's offense.

Bird was a steady point guard during her Olympic career. She consistently set up her teammates to score more than she looked for her own shot. Bird led the United States in assists in 2012 and 2021 and was second in 2016.

Taurasi is a sharpshooter. While she scores in a variety of ways, she does a lot of her damage from behind the

Diana Taurasi, *left*, and Sue Bird, *right*, also played in the WNBA.

three-point line. Taurasi led the United States in scoring at the 2012 Olympics and at the 2016 Games in Rio de Janeiro, Brazil.

When the United States took home gold at the Tokyo Games in 2021, Bird and Taurasi each won their fifth gold medal. Taurasi then went on to play in the 2024 Games at 42 years old. She became the first player to ever win six gold medals in Olympic basketball history.

AMERICAN DYNASTY

Bird and Taurasi had plenty of talented teammates during their undefeated run at the Olympics. Sylvia Fowles played in her first Olympics in 2008. The 6-foot-6 center was a rebounding force on both ends of the court. And she scored with incredible efficiency. In 27 career Olympic games, Fowles made 65 percent of her shots. After helping the United States win gold in 2021, she became one of six players to have won at least four gold medals in women's basketball.

Forward Breanna Stewart made a huge impact right away for the United States. In her Olympic debut at the 2016 Games, Stewart scored 15 points. Then she made all four of her shots in that year's gold-medal game against Spain.

The 6-foot, 4-inch Stewart could beat defenders off the dribble. And she could post up smaller opponents. Stewart also used her size for rebounding and defense. Japan made it to

Breanna Stewart averaged 15.0 points, 10.0 rebounds, and 4.7 assists at the Tokyo Olympics in 2021.

the gold-medal game on home soil at the Tokyo Olympics in 2021. But Stewart made sure the home team did not pull off the upset. On top of recording 14 points and 14 rebounds, Stewart added four steals and three blocks.

Another American superstar made her Olympic debut in Tokyo. A'ja Wilson scored 19 points and added five blocks in that year's gold-medal game. The 6-foot, 4-inch center quickly established herself as one of the world's best players.

Stewart and Wilson played together again at the 2024 Games. Like every Olympics since 1996, the United States cruised to the gold-medal game. However, France was waiting for the Americans. Playing in front of an energized home

The US women pose with their gold medals after beating France in the 2024 Olympic basketball finals.

crowd, the French slowed down the US offense. Midway through the third quarter, France led by 10 points.

Wilson had been struggling on offense throughout the game. With the gold medal slipping away, Wilson stepped it up in the second half. She blocked three shots in the third quarter. She also made her final four shot attempts of the game. Wilson finished with 21 points and 13 rebounds. The Americans outlasted France with a thrilling 67–66 win, securing their eighth straight Olympic gold medal.

GLOSSARY

amateur
A person who plays a sport without getting paid.

assists
Passes that lead directly to baskets.

boycott
To refuse to take part in an event as a form of protest.

charge
A foul when an offensive player runs into a defender who is in a set position.

commissioner
The chief executive of a sports league.

debut
First appearance.

double-double
Accumulating 10 or more of two certain statistics in a game.

elite
The highest level.

paint
The rectangular area between the free-throw line and the basket.

perimeter
In basketball, the area near the three-point line.

post
The area around the basket where power forwards and centers usually play.

screen
When an offensive player legally blocks the path of a defender to open up a teammate for a shot or a pass.

triple-double
Accumulating 10 or more of three certain statistics in a game.

underdog
The person or team that is not expected to win.

zone defense
When players guard an area of the court instead of a specific offensive player.

MORE INFORMATION

BOOKS

Giedd, Steph. *Basketball Strategies*. Abdo, 2024.

Huddleston, Emma. *Legends of Women's Basketball*. Press Box Books, 2021.

McDougall, Chrös. *The Olympics Encyclopedia*. Abdo, 2022.

ONLINE RESOURCES

Booklinks
NONFICTION NETWORK
FREE! ONLINE NONFICTION RESOURCES

To learn more about Olympic basketball, please visit **abdobooklinks.com** or scan this QR code. These links are routinely monitored and updated to provide the most current information available.

INDEX

ABOUT THE AUTHOR

Luke Hanlon is an editor and sportswriter who lives in Minneapolis, Minnesota. He grew up playing basketball and watches as many Olympic basketball games as possible every four years.